Awaiting the Glorious catch away

(1 Thessalonians 4:16-17)

By

Jennifer Nakuda

All Scripture quotations in this book are taken from the King James Version of the Bible unless otherwise indicated.

First printing 2021

Second printing 2025

USA Contact:

Tel: +1 945 304 3959

Email: jeniffern2000@gmail.com

Visit my social media:

Instagram: Jennifer Nakuda Author

Facebook: Jennifer Nakuda Author

Miracle Center Embassy

Arua, Uganda

Tel: +256 772612656, +256 703656873,

Email: franknankunda@gmail.com

Dedication

I humbly take this grand opportunity to appreciate the man of God who has had the greatest influence upon our lives and ministry through the years, Rev Chris Oyakhilome, DSc, DD. Thank you, dear man of God, for always teaching us the timeless truth of God's Word in its simplest form. Hearing you has brought out the best of God in us. I am forever grateful to God for you, Sir. I love you dearly and pray for you always.

Acknowledgments

This book wouldn't be possible without the immense inspiration of the Holy Spirit about the urgency of the hour, when you know the inevitability of the occurrence of the event and how crucial it is for everyone to be in earnest expectation. I consider it a great honor from the Spirit of God to write down these few 'look out for' as we prepare ourselves for that great day.

I'm forever grateful to the men and women of God who have been gifted to understand the times and seasons, consistently explaining Bible prophecy for everyone to come into the know of the times we are living in today. You have done your part, and like the Bible often says, "Let him that has an ear hear what the Spirit is saying to the church; everyone that has an ear will indeed hear."

A big thank you to Bookwave Publishing for a job well done in refining the words, designing the cover page, and publishing a beautiful piece of work.

And of course, a mega thank you to my dear husband, for his unwavering support always. Thank you very much.

* * *

About the Author

Jennifer Nakuda is an ordained Pastor and co-founder, alongside her husband, Frank Nakuda, of Miracle Embassy Church in Uganda, East Africa. Since 2003, she has served in various capacities within the church ministry. Inspired by her interactions with people from all walks of life, Pastor Jennifer has authored six books, offering practical guidance on living a purposeful and fulfilling Christian life. Outside of her ministry work, she is inspired by the beauty of the natural environment, enjoys traveling, and values quality time with family and friends.

Let us connect on Facebook, Instagram

or via email: jeniffern2000@gmail.com

* * *

Table of Contents

CHAPTER ONE
The rapture of the church

"And now brothers and sisters, I want you to know what will happen to the Christians who have died so you will not be full of sorrow like people who have no hope. For since we believe that Jesus died and was raised to life again, we also believe that when Jesus comes, God will bring back with Jesus all the Christians who have died. I can tell you this directly from the Lord; we who are still living when the Lord returns will not rise to meet him ahead of those who are in their graves. For the Lord himself will come down from heaven with a commanding shout, with the call of the archangel, and with the trumpet call of God. First, all the Christians who have died will rise from their graves. Then, together with them, we who are still alive and remain (i.e. the members of the body of Jesus Christ that are still alive and living for Christ) on earth will be caught up in the clouds to meet the Lord in the air and remain with him forever. So comfort and encourage each other with these words." (1 Thessalonians 4:13-18 NLT).

Dearly beloved of the Lord, the catch away of the church of Jesus Christ, popularly known as the rapture of the church, is not a debatable subject. The Scriptures vividly show that one day Jesus Christ, the savior of the world, will surely come and take away the born-again Christians who believe in him and are living for him. In the twinkling of an eye, they will be carried away from this earth to heaven to be with the Lord as particularly revealed to the apostles.

"But let me tell you a wonderful secret God has revealed to us. Not all of us will die, but we will all be transformed. It will happen in a moment, in the blinking of an eye, when the last trumpet is blown. For when the trumpet sounds, the Christians who have died will be raised with transformed bodies. And then we who are living will be transformed so that we will never die; For our perishable earthly bodies must be transformed into heavenly bodies that will never die." (1 Corinthians 15:51-53 NLT).

Since the inception of the church of Jesus Christ on the day of Pentecost, a lot has been happening as it was prophesied in the Scriptures. We know through the Scriptures that the church was given 2000 years of reigning on the earth and thereafter the millennial rule of the messiah himself from Jerusalem for 1000 years. Therefore, if the church started around 30 AD, according to church history, count how much time we could have from 1 AD.

It is important for us to always remember that Jesus' message of salvation and the kingdom of God was intended to first begin with the Jewish people, originally chosen by God and in a covenant with God. But because the Jews as a nation rejected him, the Kingdom was then brought to the nation that would produce its fruits (Matt 21:43). That nation is the Gentile nation comprised of all people in the world that are not Jews (Ephesians 2:11-13); the Gentiles are currently being invited into the kingdom through the gospel of Jesus Christ.

Apostle Paul made this clear to the Gentiles, saying, *"I want you to understand this mystery, dear brothers and sisters, so that you will not feel proud and start bragging. Some of the Jews have hard hearts, but this will last only until the complete number of Gentiles comes to Christ."* (Rom 11:25 NLT).

Jesus also mentioned the same while talking about the signs of his second coming, saying, *"...And Jerusalem will be conquered and trampled down by the Gentiles <u>until the age of the Gentiles comes to an end."</u>* (Luke 21:24 NLT).

The end of the Gentiles' age (when the gospel would have been preached to the ends of the earth and the complete number of Gentiles has come to Christ, in which period we are right now) is what will witness the rapture of the church according to the Scriptures. Then immediately after the rapture of the church comes a period already determined in which Satan will have control over the world through the man of sin, who will be given power to inflict all manner of pain and destruction on the world during his seven-year reign. (Rev 13).

The Bible says because men refused the love of the truth to be saved, *"therefore God sends upon them a misleading influence, a working of error and a strong delusion to make them believe what is false. So that all will be condemned who have not believed the truth but have delighted in wickedness."* (2 The 2:11-12).

The stage for the man of sin has been set. This is a call to every child of God to watch and pray for though rapture may take place before or after this man of sin is revealed, his deadly oppressive works are illegally coming before him, rolling out one after another, which the church must not allow in our day. But this is a mega sign that rapture is just a matter of happening any time for the Bible says in the last days evil shall abound and Satan being aware of the closing age and his fixed time of reign after the rapture, is preparing himself ahead of time and also trying to have more time of rule over the world by coming in early. The children of God should not allow this now. As long as the church of Jesus Christ is still on the earth, it is in charge, reigning through Christ. Romans 5:17, Revelation 5:10

Although the works of this antichrist are already being revealed on the earth and causing trouble to humanity more than ever, the man himself can only come into full operation when the church of Jesus Christ is taken out of here, according to the Scriptures. *"And now you know what is restraining that he may be revealed in his own time. For the mystery of lawlessness is already at work; only he who now restrains will do so until he is taken out of the way. And then the lawless one will be revealed... Even him whose coming is after the working of Satan with all power and signs and lying wonders. And with all deceivableness of unrighteousness in them that perish because they received not the love of the truth that they might be saved."* (2 Thes 2:6-10 NKJV).

Until the church is out of the earth, this man of sin cannot be in charge because it is still the church age. The church in the earth is the representation of God's presence in the earth, demonstrating power and authority through Jesus Christ, whose name was given power and authority in heaven, on earth, and under the earth. That at the mention of His name, every knee should bow, and every tongue should confess that Jesus is Lord to the glory of God the Father (Phil 2:8-11). Therefore, God and Satan cannot be in charge at the same time. The church has to be out of here first, and Satan takes full charge of the earth. In that case, the church should be strong and reign above the system and bring many to the kingdom of God in this hour.

No matter what happens, we are more than conquerors. We have the power and authority to reign in the name of Jesus and stop the wickedness in our time. This is the reason for the teaching and personal study of God's Word (Ephesians 4:11-14), so that the body of Christ comes to full maturity in Christ, taking up the responsibility to reign in the earth and bring many to the kingdom while waiting for his appearing.

Jesus is not coming back for a weak, beaten, defeated church. He is coming for a triumphant church that has so reigned and demonstrated the beauty and glory of the kingdom of heaven on earth. The church will be carried away in victory, having manifested the power and love of God in the earth for everyone to know and acknowledge the existence of the God of heaven and earth.

In the meantime, we are engaged in a critical battle of all ages that requires fearlessness and wisdom - the battle for souls. We must focus now more than ever before on winning souls to Christ. This is the reason He came, died, and rose again so that men will not perish with Satan in the final judgment. He has committed to us the ministry of reconciling men back to him (2 Cor 5: 18). All the power and authority we have on this earth is for this sole purpose – to let all people know about His love and saving grace.

Israel's last generation is a major sign

There is enough evidence in the world today to prove the impending rapture of the church. All the mega prophetic signs in the Bible are happening in our day. From the restoration of the nation of Israel in 1948 to the declaration of Jerusalem as its capital in 2018 at their 70th-year celebration and the current plans to rebuild the temple, one can only say that our time is surely up. Seeing that this is the generation of the Jews which the Lord said will not pass away till all prophecy on Israel is fulfilled (Luke 21:32) and knowing that a generation of this kind runs for 100 years, one can only watch and pray as Jesus cautioned us. For no one knows the day or the hour. According to Jesus, this generation doesn't have to end first. In other words, every prophecy is fulfilled within this generation of the Jewish nation.

Therefore, if all prophecies on Israel must be fulfilled within this present Jewish generation, then this means that the antichrist will be revealed in this generation to reign for seven years on earth, having his headquarters in the Jewish capital Jerusalem. At the end of his seven-year reign, precisely after the great tribulation of those days, shall be the second coming of Christ with His saints that were taken during the rapture. (Jude 1:14-15).

When talking to the Jews about the signs of his second coming at the end of time, Jesus particularly said, ***"When ye, therefore, shall see the abomination of desolation spoken of by Daniel the prophet stand in the holy place, (whosoever reads let him understand)"*** (Matt 24:15). The abomination of desolation was revealed to Daniel while praying for Israel and the holy land.

Prophet Daniel received understanding from Angel Gabriel about Israel and the holy land in the end times (Dan 9:20-27). The Angel specifically told Daniel about one who will make a covenant with Israel for seven weeks (which is seven years) and then break it halfway to stop the sacrifices in the temple so he can put up a blasphemous object to be worshipped instead of the living God.

"He will make a treaty with the people for a period of one set of seven, but after half this time he will put an end to the sacrifices and offerings. Then as a climax to all his terrible deeds, he will set up a sacrilegious object that causes desecration, until the end that has been decreed is poured out on this defiler." (Dan 9:27 NLT).

This is the abomination that Jesus was warning them of. As soon as they see this happening, they should flee to the mountains because it will henceforth be a time of trouble like the world has never seen before, and neither will it see it again. *"For then shall be great tribulation such as was not since the beginning of the world to this time, nor ever shall be. And except those days should be shortened, there should no flesh be saved but for the elect's sake those days shall be shortened."* (Matt 24:21-22).

Of course, the one who will sign the treaty with the people of Israel for seven years is the antichrist, who will assure them of peace and guarantee their safety in the Middle East. But halfway into the treaty, he will break it; having moved his headquarters into Jerusalem, he will demand to be worshipped above every other God. *"Who opposes and exalts himself above all that is called God or that is worshipped so that he as God sits in the temple of God, showing himself that he is God."*(2 Thess 2:4).

When he shall have set up the abomination in the holy place to be worshipped instead of God (Matt 24:15), a great and terrible tribulation will break out, demanding everyone to worship his image. This then will be followed by the second coming of Christ *"Immediately after the tribulation of those days shall the sun be darkened and the moon shall not give her light and the stars shall fall from heaven and the powers of the heavens shall be shaken, And then shall appear the sign of the son of man in heaven and then shall all the tribes of the earth mourn and they shall see the Son of man coming in the clouds of heaven with power and great glory."* (Matt 24:29-31).

During the great tribulation, the Jews will cry out to the Lord God for help: *"Come and let us return unto the Lord for he has torn and he will heal us; he has smitten and he will bind us up. After two days will he revive us; in the third day he will raise us up and we shall live in his sight."* (Hosea 6:1-2). As Hosea saw, the Lord will come to their rescue, and they will live in His sight on the third day, which is the millennial reign of the Messiah (Jesus Christ) will begin at his second coming.

Understand this, that after the two days (two thousand years) of the church age, when the 'ready Christians' have been raptured from the earth, the Jews will be revived by the message of the two witnesses who will preach to the whole world for three and half years during the seven years of the antichrist according to Revelation 11. And when he finally comes, they will live in his sight on the third day of the millennial rule. For one day is as a thousand years in his sight (2 Peter 3:8).

At his second coming, he will come with his saints in power and great glory to execute judgment and at the same time commence his millennial rule in Jerusalem. *"And Enoch also the seventh from Adam prophesied of these saying, behold the lord cometh with ten thousands of his saints. To execute judgment upon all and to convince all that are ungodly among them of all their ungodly deed which they have ungodly committed and of all their hard speeches which ungodly sinners have spoken against him."* (Jude 1:14-15) (Zech14).

Why you should be raptured

By now, we should know that the rapture of the church will first take place before the second coming of Jesus Christ to begin the millennial reign. As a member of the body of Christ, the church of Jesus Christ, the rapture is happening for you. It was prepared and planned for you and not any other group. This calls for conscious preparation for every child of God, as rapture could take place any time from now, according to the Scriptures.

Another very strong reason why you should be raptured is the fact that at rapture, our time as the church of Jesus Christ will be over on earth. You have no business staying here because immediately after the rapture, a new season will follow, and you will have no power because it is a season determined for Satan to have power over the earth. The Bible says, *"The beast was given a mouth to utter proud words and blasphemies and to exercise his authority for forty-two months. He opened his mouth to blaspheme God and to slander his name and his dwelling place and those who live in heaven. He was given the power to make war against the saints and to conquer them. And he was given authority over every tribe, people language, and nation. All inhabitants of the earth will worship the beast – all whose names have not been written in the Book of Life belonging to the Lamb that was slain from the creation of the world. He who has an ear let him hear. If anyone is to go into captivity, into captivity he will go. If anyone is to be killed with the sword, with the sword he will be killed. This calls for the patient endurance and faithfulness on the part of the saints."* (Rev 13:5-10 NIV).

Satan, through the antichrist, will inflict pain on all that dwell on the earth, including the saints of God who will be in the earth after the rapture. For their testimony of Jesus, some saints will be thrown into prison to die from torture, while others will be tortured to death right away. You don't have to go through this. All it takes to escape this period of terrible trouble to come is living for Him now in readiness for the rapture. After explaining to the people all the trouble that would take place in those days, Jesus cautioned us, saying, *"Be always on the watch, and pray that you may be able to escape all that is about to happen and that you may be able to stand before the son of man."* (Luke 21:36).

Rapture is so important to us as the church of Jesus Christ for being our final victory and fulfillment of Scripture. The Bible says. *"For when the trumpet sounds, the Christians who have died will be raised with transformed bodies. And then we who are living will be transformed so that we will never die. For our perishable earthly bodies must be transformed into heavenly* bodies *that will never die. When this happens, when our perishable bodies have been transformed into heavenly bodies that will never die, then at last the scripture will come true: 'Death is swallowed up in victory.' O death where is your victory? O death where is your sting"*. (1 Corinthians 15: 51-55 NLT).

Another beautiful reason you should be raptured is to honor your invitation to the marriage supper of the lamb by going first flight, as my pastor calls it; you don't want to dare the tribulation period. The Bible lets us know in Rev 19:1-9 that there is going to be a marriage supper of the Lamb in heaven in which a great multitude of his saints, both great and small, will gather to rejoice and give him honor.

The angel that revealed this to John specifically told him to write, *"Blessed are they which are called unto the marriage supper of the lamb. And he saith unto me, these are the true sayings of God"*. All the saints of God will be at the marriage supper of the Lamb. Those who have gone before, the rapture saints and the tribulation saints who will be killed for their testimony of Jesus, will all be gathered for this great feast in honor of the Lamb. It will be a great time of rejoicing and celebration in heaven.

Immediately after the celebration of those days, will the King of Kings and Lord of Lords mount His white horse for His second coming on the earth with great power and glory, His saints with him, to execute judgment and make war. *"And I saw heaven opened and behold a white a horse and him that sat upon him was called Faithful and True, and in righteousness, he doth judge and make war. His eyes were as a flame of fire, and on his head were many crowns, and he had a name written, that no man knew, but he himself. And he was clothed with a vesture dipped in blood: and his name is called the Word of God. And the armies which were in heaven followed him upon white horses. Clothed in fine linen, white and clean. Out of his mouth goes a sharp sword, that with it he should smite the nations: and he shall rule them with a rod of iron: and he treads the winepress of the fierceness and wrath of Almighty God. And he has on his vesture and his thigh a name written KING OF KINGS AND LORD OF LORDS.*

And I saw an angel standing in the sun; and he cried with a loud voice, saying to all the fowls that fly in the midst of heaven, come and gather yourselves together unto the supper of the great God. That ye may eat the flesh of kings, and the flesh of captains, and the flesh of mighty men, and the flesh of horses and of them that sit on them, and the flesh of all men, both free and bond, both small and great. And I saw the beast and the kings of the earth, and their armies, gathered together to make war against him that sat on the horse, and against his army. And the beast was taken, and with him the false prophet that wrought miracles before him, with which he deceived them that had received the mark of the beast, and them that worshipped his image. These both were cast alive into the lake of fire burning with brimstone. And the remnant were slain with the sword of him that sat upon the horse, which sword proceeded out of his mouth; and all the fowls were filled with their flesh." (Rev 19: 11-21). And so that will be the end of the Antichrist era when all of them that deceived and those that were deceived will be destroyed, and the earth cleansed of the evil, then the millennium will begin with Jesus' reigning in the earth.

Everyone ready for the rapture will hear the trumpet, and at the sound of that trumpet, we will be changed and caught away from this earth. The rest of the world will try to figure out what happened to the Christians, but will have no answers. Only those Christians who were not ready will know what exactly would have happened at the time. I can imagine just like Enoch, who walked with God and was no more. No one saw him go, but they knew God took him, for he was not found anywhere. (Hebrews 11:5).

Jesus said, like the days of Noah, so shall the coming of the Son of man be. *"For as in the days that were before the flood they were eating and drinking, marrying and giving in marriage, until the day that Noah entered into the ark. And knew not until the flood came, and took them all away; so, shall also be the coming of the Son of man be. Then shall two be in the field; the one shall be taken, and the other left. Two women shall be grinding at the mill; the one shall be taken, and the other left. Watch; therefore, for ye know not what hour your Lord does come. But know this; if the goodman of the house had known in what watch the thief would come, he would have watched and would not have suffered his house to be broken up. Therefore, be ye also ready; for in such an hour as ye think not the son of man cometh."* (Matt 24:39-44). Don't be the good man of the house who might be found unprepared for his coming.

* * *

CHAPTER TWO

The church without spot or wrinkle

While we all await his glorious appearance now more than ever, we need to refocus all our energies on getting ourselves ready. This we do by looking into the Scriptures to find out the kind of saints he will be taking with him on that day. And like any wise person, to make sure we are that saint, He is coming back to take.

While advising husbands to love their wives, Apostle Peter gave a comparison to what Jesus did for the church, saying, *"Husbands love your wives even as Christ also loved the Church and gave himself for it. that he might sanctify and <u>cleanse it with the washing of water by the word</u>, that he might present it to himself a glorious church not having spot or wrinkle or any such thing; but that it should be holy and without blemish."* (Ephesians 5:25-27).

Now, that spotless, without blemish or wrinkle church that Jesus purified for himself with the washing of water by the word is the very one that he is coming back for. Someone may ask, Is it possible to be found spotless? Emphatically yes! That is what he did when we gave him our hearts (he made us spotless) and gave us his word to teach us how to live and remain spotless, without blemish.

The Bible is not a book for preachers to get sermons for the pulpit. It was given to each one of us primarily to know God, to know who we have become in Christ, and to know how to live this righteous and glorious life of God given to us. It is a must-study book for every serious Christian who desires to live for the Lord. It is our instruction manual for life.

We are washed, sanctified, and justified

"Do you not know that the unrighteous will not inherit the kingdom of God? Do not be deceived. Neither fornicators, nor idolaters, nor adulterers, nor homosexuals, nor sodomites, thieves, nor covetous, nor drunkards, nor revilers, nor extortionists will inherit the kingdom of God. And such were some of you; but ye are washed, but ye are sanctified, but ye are justified in the name of the Lord Jesus and by the Spirit of our God." (1 Corinthians 6:11 NIV). Glory hallelujah! Did you see that? We are not working on being washed, nor are we working on becoming spotless or blameless. Rather, we are washed; we are sanctified (made holy); we are justified (vindicated, accepted, declared not guilty). It is our responsibility to remain so just like Apostle Peter advised all those who are looking forward to His coming saying, *"So then, dear friends since you are looking forward to this, make every effort to be found spotless, blameless, and at peace with him."* (2 Peter 3:14 NIV).

When we accepted Christ as Lord of our lives, God gave us His very own eternal life and nature of righteousness, plus His Holy Spirit and His Word to enable us to live a life that is spotless, blameless, and at peace with Him. We are not in Christ trying to live a holy life, we live a holy life in Christ, and we are expected to; because of who we are – children of God with the life and nature of God. Every child of God has to come to the acknowledgment of what we have in Christ and who we are made of; and know for sure that sin has no power over us. We were brought into God's class. We are participators in the divine nature (2 Peter 1:4).

In us is the ability to put away everything that hinders us and the sin that easily besets us, just like those who have gone before us. *"Therefore, since we are surrounded by such a great cloud of witnesses, let us throw off everything that hinders and the sin that so easily entangles and let us run with perseverance the race marked out for us. Let us fix our eyes on Jesus the author and perfecter of our faith who for the joy set before him endured the cross scorning its shame and sat down at the right hand of the throne of God. Consider him who endured such opposition from sinful men, so that you will not grow weary and lose heart. In your struggle against sin, you have not yet resisted to the point of shedding your blood."* (Heb 12:1-4 NIV).

In Christ, we are recreated, born anew after God in righteousness and true holiness. ***And that ye put on the new man which after God is created in righteousness and true holiness."*** (Eph 4:24). This nature of righteousness imparted to our spirits makes it possible for us to walk in righteousness. *"This I say therefore and testify in the Lord that ye henceforth walk not as other gentiles walk in the vanity of their minds; having the understanding darkened, being alienated from the life of God through the ignorance that is in them because of the blindness of their heart; who being past feeling have given themselves over unto lasciviousness to work all uncleanness with greediness. But ye have not so learned Christ; if so be that ye have heard him and have been taught by him as the truth is* *in Jesus; that ye put off concerning the former conversation (manner of life), the old man which is corrupt according to the deceitful lusts; and be renewed in the spirit of your mind;* (Ephesians 4:17-23).

It is because of this new nature of righteousness in us that John, by the Spirit, lets us know that we cannot sin because God's seed is in us. ***"Whosoever is born of God does not commit sin, for his seed remains in him and he cannot sin because he is born of God."*** (1 John 3:9). The nature of righteousness in our spirits produces in us love, joy, and peace, longsuffering, gentleness, goodness, faith, meekness, self-control by the Holy Spirit of God. The Bible says against these, there's no law because they are the fruit of our recreated human spirit; they are in our spirit; we walk in them naturally. No one needs to tell us to walk in them. We choose to make them our way of life. It is a decision we make personally. (Gal 5:16-26).

Righteousness is the life we live in Christ. It guides our path, eliminating errors in our journey. A Christian will sin for not knowing the Scriptures or refusing to live according to the Scriptures. Jesus said, ***"ye do err, not knowing the scriptures or the power of God."*** (Matt 22:29). He didn't say you err because you are human, but because you don't know the Scriptures or the power of God. This is what King David knew when he said, ***"Thy word have I hid in mine heart, that I might not sin against thee."*** (Psalms 119:11). The Word of God was given to us to train us in the life of righteousness. (2 Tim 3:16-17). If you make the Word of God your life companion, it will guide you on the path of righteousness naturally.

The world as it is has been so corrupted, and the enemy of Christ is so desperately wicked that he will do anything for you to lose your salvation. But God has brought us into fellowship with Himself and given us His Word to live by. If we keep our eyes on the Word of God, we create our atmosphere filled with the light of God's Word, and the Bible says, in that light, the blood of Jesus Christ automatically cleanses us from any spot, blemish, or sin that tries to fasten itself on us. *"If we say that we have fellowship with him and walk in darkness we lie and do not the truth. But if we walk in the light as he is in the light we have fellowship one with another and the blood of Jesus Christ his Son cleanses us from all sin."* (1 John1:6-7).

Jesus, while talking to his disciples, said, *"Now ye are clean through the word which I have spoken unto you"* (John 15:3), letting us know that the word is a perfect cleanser. Every time we study and hear the word, it washes away every blemish, trying to contaminate our minds knowingly or unknowingly.

Take, for example, how you could feel after watching global or local news that makes the future look hopeless. You will need to get to the Word of God to wash your mind before you begin to think and speak fear or uncertainty. The Word of God will not only wash you, but it will also build your faith strong in the Lord; to remain steadfast no matter what happens to you or around you.

It is pretty obvious that as we wait for his appearance, there is a consciousness we ought to have that shows our readiness for the master. There is definitely a way of life that we should awaken to now more than before. A kind of life that lives every day in anticipation of rapture, awaiting the glorious catch away.

The Bible says, *"As ye have therefore received Christ Jesus the Lord, so walk ye in him; rooted and built up in him and established in the faith, as ye have been taught, abounding therein with thanksgiving. Beware lest any man spoils you through philosophy and vain deceit, after the tradition of men, after the rudiments (the principles) of the world, and not after Christ.* (Colossians 2:6-8).

* * *

CHAPTER THREE

Owing nothing but love

As we wait, one of the key things that we must watch out for and committedly yield to and willingly allow to flow from our spirit is the love of God that has been poured out into our hearts by the Holy Spirit (Rom5:5). This is no time to wait to be loved or treated well first. This is the time to let love flow from your spirit to the world around you. Do not let your love be quenched by the evil around you. Let love stand out. It is one of the strongest attributes of the recreated human spirit, and a weapon given to us in our mission to the hurting world. It was given to us to love even the most unlovable, you know.

"Owe no man anything but to love one another for he that loves another has fulfilled the law. For this, thou shalt not commit adultery; thou shalt not kill; thou shalt not steal; thou shalt not bear false witness; thou shalt not covet; and if there be any other commandments, it is briefly comprehended in this saying, namely thou shalt love thy neighbor as thyself. Love works no ill to his neighbor; therefore love is the fulfillment of the law. And that knowing the time, that now it is high time to awake out of sleep for now is our salvation nearer than when we believed. The night is far spent, the day is at hand; lets us therefore cast off the works of darkness and let us put on the armor of light." (Romans 13:8-14).

The Spirit is saying we should owe no man anything apart from love, as we see our time closing up. We should put off the deeds of darkness and be the light we are to our world through love. Love is not impossible for a child of God (1 John 4:7-8). Love is a spiritual force that flows from our recreated human spirit to the outside world. Love does not consider the evil or the emptiness it encounters; it simply flows and fills the atmosphere with its sweet presence until it takes over the environment. Love manifests in good works of righteousness that minister the love of God to the hurting world.

The Spirit of God perfectly defines love for us, saying, *"Love is patient, love is kind. It does not envy, it does not boast, it is not proud. It is not rude, it is not self-seeking, it is not easily angered, and it keeps no record of wrongs. Love does not delight in evil but rejoices with the truth. It always protects, always trusts, always hopes, and always perseveres. Love never fails. But where there are prophecies, they will cease; where there are tongues; they will be stilled where there is knowledge, it will pass away… And now these three remain: faith, hope, and love. But the greatest of these is love."* (1 Corinthians 13:4-8 NIV).

Dearly Beloved of God it is in our power to let this unconditional love of God flow from us to the world around us. It is a decision we make despite the evil in our world. It is our calling to walk in love. We are children of a love God. We are just like our father God, walking in love is our life. Don't allow the multiplicity of wickedness to quench your love. Jesus warned us of many people's love growing cold in the last days because of too much wickedness. (Matt 24:12-13).

Apostle Paul reechoes the same words of Jesus, saying, *"You should also know this that in the last days, there will be very difficult times. For people will love only themselves and their money. They will be boastful and proud, scoffing at God, disobedient to their parents, and ungrateful. They will consider nothing sacred. They will be unloving and unforgiving; they will slander others and have no self-control; they will be cruel and have no interest in what is good. They will betray their friends, be reckless, be puffed up with pride, and love pleasure rather than God. They will act as if they are religious, but they will reject the power that could make them godly. You must stay away from people like that."* (2 Tim 3:1-5 NLT).

The Spirit says, stay away from such people. Don't copy them and make no friends with them because they will corrupt your good spirit. (1 Cor 15:33-34). It is called loving from afar! If you keep company with them, your mind will be flooded with wrong influence void of true knowledge, and soon you will be talking their talk and going in their direction.

Interestingly, such people are not far from us; they are very close in our circles. In verses seven and eight of chapter three, Second Timothy lets us know that they are "ever learning and never able to come to the knowledge of the truth. They are men of corrupt minds who resist the truth." But the Scripture says in verse nine, they will go no further, for soon their folly will be revealed to everyone by their fruits. Watch out for their fruits to know who they really are. Don't fall prey to their hypocrisy, listen keenly to what they say and do, and keep your guard.

Didn't Jesus tell us in the parable of the weeds that, *"The kingdom of heaven is likened unto a man who sowed good seeds in his field; but while men slept, his enemy came and sowed tares among the wheat and went his way. But when the blade was sprung up, and brought forth fruit, then appeared the tares also. So the servants of the householder came and said unto him, Sir, didn't thou sow good seed in thy field? From whence then has it tares? He said unto them, an enemy has done this. The servants said unto him wilt thou then that we go and gather them up? But he said Nay; lest while ye gather up the tares, ye root up also the wheat with them. Let both grow together until the harvest and in the time of harvest I will say to the reapers, gather ye together first the tares, and bind them in bundles to burn them; but gather the wheat into my barn."* (Matt 13:24-30).

Have you seen that? The tares were revealed at the time of bearing fruit. All the while, the servants thought it was only a garden of wheat until the fruits came out. The Bible says we shall know them by their fruits. ***"A good tree cannot bring forth evil fruit neither can a corrupt tree bring forth good fruit."*** (Matt 7:16-20).

Jesus said they were planted by the enemy of God, and their end is revealed. We should not copy their way of life simply because they seem religious and are always in our gatherings, and sometimes talk like godly men and women. We should not make them close associates as much as they are in our midst. Do them good and don't copy their way of life. Let the Word of God be your guiding light in the affairs of life, not the experiences of men. And in love guide those that in ignorance are being misled by the "tares". By doing this, you would have saved a soul from destruction.

Love is our confidence before the Father

"We know that we have passed from death unto life because we love the brethren. He that loves not his brother abides in death. Whosoever hates his brother is a murderer, and ye know that no murderer has eternal life abiding in him. Hereby perceive we the love of God because he laid down his life for us, and we ought to lay down our lives for the brethren. But whoso has this world's good, and sees his brother have a need, and shuts up his bowels of compassion from him, how dwells the love of God in him. My little children let us not love in word, neither in tongue; but in deed and in truth. And hereby we know that we are of the truth and shall assure our hearts before him." (1 John 3:14-19).

Our love should not be in words only, but in truth and good deeds, just as Jesus laid down his life for us, he expects us to love others sacrificially, considering them before ourselves, and to forego our own interests, rights, and privileges for their sake. Just wondering, when did we last give up what we loved dearly so that another person could enjoy it? Perhaps not so recent, but that's how to live a higher life where one is detached from worldly things and free from selfishness.

Love will cause us to give away what we love most, without expecting anything in return. Walking in love brings us into a closer walk with the Lord, to the extent that what men cry out to God to give them, you receive without asking because you have learned the secret of greatness – give and it shall be given unto you (Luke 6:38).

Love is the light that drives out darkness

"Let your light so shine before men, that they may see your good works and glorify your Father which is in Heaven." (Matt 5:16). God has made His children the light to dispel darkness and bring radiance in the world. Darkness represents all the evils, pains, sorrows, penury, and ignorance that surround humanity. He says, let your light so shine that the world will see your good works and glorify your father in heaven. If we are to let our light shine so much as to remove the pain and the ignorance in the world, it will have to be through love. Our light shines through our demonstration of love. The world can only see and enjoy our light through our good deeds of love that remove pain, sorrow, and penury, turning mourning into joy and hope.

Love makes the world a better place to live in and makes it possible for many to see our God and accept Him as their Lord and Savior. God demonstrated His great love for sinful man by sending His son to save and not condemn. There had never been such a strong light that hit the earth, like the light of God that shone so ever brightly through the work of the cross and the supernatural resurrection that brought us into the new life. That unconditional love is the pillar and foundation of the Christian faith. The hallmark of our Christianity. Therefore, every genuine Christian walks in love. We love without limit, not because they are good and lovable, but because that's who we are - love children of a love God.

"No one has seen God at any time. If we love one another, God abides in us and his love has been perfected in us… if someone says "I love God" and hates his brother, he is a liar; for he who does not love his brother whom he has seen, how can he love

God whom he has not seen? And this commandment have we from him, that he who loves God love his brother also." (1 John 4:7-21).

"*He that loves his brother abides in the light and there is none occasion of stumbling in him. But he that hates his brother is in darkness and walks in darkness and knows not whither he goes because that darkness has blinded his eyes.*" (1 John 2:11). "*By this shall all men know that ye are my disciples, if ye have love one to another.*" (John 13:35). "*As we have therefore opportunity let us do good unto all men, especially unto them who are of the household of faith.*" (Galatians 6:10).

* * *

CHAPTER FOUR

Be as wise as serpents and calm as doves

In our preparation for the glorious catch away, we should more than ever before be mindful of the fact that we are on a mission to bring others into the kingdom. You are not going alone. Your family and friends are a priority, as well as your neighbors and those in your sphere of contact. Do not let anybody you know live in ignorance of this truth that will surely come upon the whole earth. He did not send us because they are going to be kind to us, and easily believe our message, no, not all of them will be kind and nice. Therefore, He said, *"Behold I send you forth as sheep in the midst of wolves; be ye therefore wise as serpents, and harmless as doves."* (Matthew 10:16).

Firstly, the master says, 'I send you', which is very important for us to always remember we are on a mission here on earth until he comes. The master is counting on us to do a clean job of letting everyone in our world know about his saving grace. Although in this particular portion of Scripture, Jesus was specifically sending his twelve disciples to the house of Israel, we must understand that he eventually did send all of us who have believed in him; calling us ministers of reconciliation (2Cor 5:18). And the mode of operation has not changed; we are still as sheep sent amid wolves.

He says, go preach the kingdom, heal the sick, raise the dead, and cast out demons freely you have received the power freely give (Matt 10:7-8). We must understand that this commission has become more urgent than when it was first given. If there is anything that needs the church's topmost attention now is the preaching of the gospel of Jesus Christ as we close the church age.

This is no time to wait for the great evangelist to visit our town. The master could appear before the evangelist shows up. It is time to get to the field and quickly harvest the souls of men because they are more than ready and just waiting for someone to explain this saving gospel of Christ. Jesus said, ***"The harvest truly is plenteous, but the laborers are few"*** (Matt 10:37). Don't let this be true in your city. Become one of the laborers of the kingdom today. For some, it might require you to go back to your hometown or even your family to preach the kingdom of God and get them in before it's too late.

Secondly, the Scripture says, 'Be wise as serpents and calm as doves' while you go amid wolves. This is to let us know that our mission is to unfriendly circumstances, but we are forewarned to be wise as serpents and harmless as doves to have a successful mission.

Apostle Paul, by the Spirit, throws more light on the same warning in Ephesians 5:15-17, saying, ***"Be very careful then how you live, not as unwise but as wise, making the most of every opportunity because the days are evil. Therefore, do not be foolish, but understand what the Lord's will is."***

The Spirit wants us to be extremely careful about how we live amidst wolves. Wolves are naturally hostile to the sheep, which describes the likely hostility from the children of darkness to the children of light. We must understand that the evil spirits of darkness operating through the children of darkness will not give the children of light a smooth ride to accomplish the mission. But if we are wise and understand what God wants us to do in every situation, we will stay on course successfully.

How to act wisely on the mission

Apostle Paul, speaking to Timothy, a young pastor, reminded him that one thing that was able to make him wise, saying, *"And that from a child thou has known the holy scriptures which are able to make thee wise unto salvation through faith which is in Christ Jesus. All scripture is given by inspiration of God and is profitable for doctrine for reproof for correction for instruction in righteousness; that the man of God may be perfect thoroughly furnished unto all good works."* (2 Tim 3:15-17).

God has given us His Word to know His will in every situation and be able to walk in wisdom. The mission we are sent to requires no assumptions if we are to avoid casualties. We are therefore instructed to give ourselves to the Word to learn how to deal wisely. The more of God's Word in us, the more it forms in us the wisdom of the righteous, knowing what to do, when to do what we have to do, where and how to do it.

Apostle John affirms the importance of God's Word in guiding our lives, saying, *"The word of God is the <u>only true light</u> that lights every man that comes into this world."* (John 1:9). His word is our guiding light, showing us the path of life. For example, in 2 Peter 1:3-11, the word clearly lets us know what to do in order to be effective and productive in our walk with the Lord. In other words, what we ought to do if we are going to successfully present the gospel in all situations.

He says, *"For this very reason, make every effort to add to your faith goodness; and to goodness, knowledge; and to knowledge, self-control; and to self-control, perseverance; and to perseverance, godliness; and to godliness, brotherly kindness; and to brotherly kindness; love; For if you possess these qualities in increasing measure, they will keep you from being ineffective and unproductive in your knowledge of our Lord Jesus Christ. But if anyone does not have them, he is nearsighted and blind and has forgotten that he has been cleansed from his past sins. Therefore, my brothers, be all the more eager to make your calling and election sure. For if you do these things, you will never fail; and you will receive a rich welcome into the eternal kingdom of our Lord and Savior Jesus Christ."*

He says to make every effort to **add goodness to your faith**. Even when the occasion does not call for goodness, just be good and calm because that is being harmless as doves. We should train ourselves to be good-hearted all the time, not only when the environment is favorable and everyone is nice to us.

Our goodness should come from a pure heart, always looking out for the good of others first and wishing everyone well. Remember, we are the heirs of God; nothing could ever be taken from us to make us disadvantaged. Absolutely nothing! Therefore, let us be good in all situations because we have nothing to lose but everything to give and a crown of glory to receive at the end from the master. A simple smile or a greeting can brighten someone's day and even lead to their salvation.

He says to goodness add knowledge, especially knowledge of God's Word. Refuse to be ignorant, especially of God's Word. He says, ***"My people perish***

for lack of knowledge" (Hosea 4:6). Therefore, acquire knowledge of God's Word at all costs. Secondly, the knowledge of those things that concern us mostly in our assignment, so that we will never be at a disadvantage in our mission. What is it that God has called you to do? Is it a ministry? Get to know how the ministry works. Are you in any profession or career? First, you must know that you are there as a kingdom representative, and the kingdom has your back. You are sent there to showcase the excellence of our kingdom and the expertise of the Spirit.

We are mandated to teach the nations how to live. Therefore, we learn what they do and then cream it with the wisdom from our kingdom and take over in that profession, career, industry, sector, or field. We are sent to demonstrate excellence and expertise like Daniel in Babylon (Daniel 2:46-49) and Joseph in Egypt (Genesis 41:38-43). Have knowledge of how things work in your area of operation. Don't be the one that they can easily replace. Don't live on assumptions, understand the will of God, and you will be able to touch and impact many lives.

To knowledge, the spirit says to add self-control. Just because you know something and you are right, it does not mean, every time is just perfect to speak out or act. Self-control, which is the ability to hold yourself in, will help you stay quiet when you have to and speak or act wisely when you have to, making you harmless as a dove. Self-control will help you understand the situation better, enabling you to respond wisely and escape many snares and traps that are set up by the enemy.

You can't afford to live without self-control; it is a strong weapon in conquering the lust of the flesh and the obvious temptations aiming at destroying your life (1 John 2:15-17). It will help you get rid of anger. Being hot-tempered is not godly, regardless of the circumstance. It will rob you of many blessings in your Christian journey, and you surely don't want to miss out on that rich welcome into the eternal kingdom of our Lord and Savior Jesus Christ.

To self-control, he says add patience, which will keep you in God's perfect peace. Patience will allow the peace of God to mount guard over your heart while you watch for the physical manifestation of those things you prayed for and received a note of victory. Rejoicing patiently will keep your heart in perfect peace instead of worrying over the same issue again and again.

Patience will help you avoid grave mistakes in life, which appear as grand opportunities of a lifetime, yet they are traps leading to destruction. It will teach you to be grateful for many things in life. It will teach you how to trust God, knowing that He who called you is faithful to see you through and to accomplish that which He started in and around you. Patience will enable you to understand and help many people in trying moments of their lives.

He says to patience add godliness, which is the outward expression of your inner devotion to God. You can't live in a place and people find it difficult to call you a Christian. Godliness is devoutly displayed in a person's way of life. Profane and inappropriate character corrupts a person's spirituality. Just everything can't be of interest to you. You must have something you stand for and be known for, something of value to you, something that you give the highest priority in life.

Paul said, *"I am made all things to all men that I might by all means save some. And this I do for the gospel's sake"* (1 Corinthians 9:22-23). Everything that Paul became and did wherever he went was for the sole purpose of winning people's hearts to Christ, and he did not allow any of the things he did to sabotage his godliness. He knew who he was and how far to go. For he had earlier said, *"All things are lawful for me, but not all things are helpful; all things are lawful for me, but I will not be brought under the power of any"* (1 Corinthians 6:12) our way of life ought to display the kind of godliness that attracts others to Christ not repelling them.

To godliness, he says add brotherly kindness, which is an open show of compassion towards others. Many will not care just how much godly you may be until you show how much you're concerned about them. Kindheartedness will help you understand everyone's situation and know how to reach out to them. Many have received Christ as a result of our kind gestures, like the help we have extended when they were in need. And many have been restored to the faith because we were just kind and understanding. Kindness is one component of love that can never fail to touch a person's heart.

To brotherly kindness add love, which is the greatest of all. Love is everything good and pure in life, according to 1 Corinthians 13. Love will move you to do the seemingly impossible, breaking barriers and bridges. The love of God poured into our hearts by the Holy Spirit is one of the greatest weapons given to us for a most effective and productive life. Love humbles the hardest of hearts. Just let it out and watch the impact you will make without limits. May people meet us, and all they ever remember about us be the love of Christ they saw in us.

The Scripture has boldly said, if you have these qualities in increasing measure, they will keep you from being ineffective and unproductive; you will surely never fail. Above all, you will receive a rich welcome into the eternal kingdom of our Lord and Savior Jesus Christ.

Daniel 12:3 assures us of the incomparable glory hereafter of those who act wisely in this life. *"And they that be wise shall shine as the brightness of the firmament, and they that turn many to righteousness as the stars forever and ever"*.

* * *

CHAPTER FIVE

Fearless and very courageous

"He that overcomes shall inherit all things, and I will be his God, and he shall be my son. <u>But the fearful and unbelieving,</u> and the abominable and murderers and whoremongers, and sorcerers and idolaters and all liars shall have their part in the lake which burns with fire and brimstone; which is the second death." (Revelation 21:7-8).

Looking at the category of characters among which God places fear, and unbelief is evident enough to tell us that fear is not something to joke about. It is not only dangerous to one's life here on earth, but can also cost someone a great future with God!

As we wait for the glorious catch away, we must, of necessity, be very bold and very courageous, having absolute trust in the Lord of our salvation. These are the times when Daniel said, ***"But the people that do know their God shall be strong and do exploits."*** (Dan 11:32).

This is the time to know who we are and cling to the truth of God's Word regardless of the situation. These are the last days, and wickedness is at its highest with the sole purpose of drowning all that is good. The workers of iniquity are very bold, carrying out their evil deeds without remorse in broad daylight just to make everyone accept their evil ways as the norm.

Jesus said in the last days iniquity shall abound, but he that endures to the end shall be saved. (Matt 24: 12-13). This is no time to fear or worry about anything. The Bible says, ***"Be anxious for nothing but in everything by prayer and supplication with thanksgiving let your requests be known unto God. And the peace of God, which passes all understanding, shall keep your hearts and minds through Christ Jesus."*** (Philippians 4:6-7).

To be anxious means that you believe that your fears may actually come to pass, and through anxiety, you imagine your fears to be real. And because our imaginative ability is our creative ability, you make your fears a reality by being anxious.

Fear creates a negative force around you that attracts what you fear to come to you. That's why God doesn't want you to fear, because fear empowers what you fear to become real. God wants you to let His peace keep your heart and mind through faith in Him.

Fear is of the devil, and he has always used it to rob many of their victory, blessings, and life itself. Allowing fear to overwhelm you means walking away from victory to defeat. Time and again in the Bible, God warns us about fear because of its ability to destroy destiny, purpose, and life.

It doesn't matter what is happening around you in this world today; you are not of this world, and greater is he that is in you than he that is in the world. (1Jn 4:4). Have no fear of anything in this life. Give the devil no place at all in your life (Eph 4:27), resist fear and fear will flee (James 4:7). God has assured us in His Word that we are more than conquerors in all these things through Him that loved us. (Rom 8:37).

The Spirit of power, love, and a sound mind

Paul writing to Timothy his son reminded him of how to take advantage of the gift of God in him saying, *"Wherefore I put thee in remembrance that thou stir up the gift of God which is in thee... For God has not given us the spirit of fear but of power and of love and of a sound mind."* (2Tim 2:5-6).

This portion of Scripture is very instructive! Letting us know that the Spirit of God in us is not of fear but power, love, and a sound mind. This actually means the gift of God in us; who is the Holy Spirit, is the Spirit of power in us; he is the Spirit of love in us, and he is the Spirit of a sound mind in us. Every time we come in contact with a terrifying and worrying situation, God expects us to take advantage of the presence of the Holy Spirit in us and turn on the power (Acts 1:8), the love (1 John4:18), or the wisdom (Isa 11:2) as the need of the hour may require; instead of entertaining fear or worry.

This literary tells us that we have all we require to solve life's problems instead of giving way to fear. If the situation requires a demonstration of the power of God, the Spirit of God in us is the power of God. If the situation requires a display of love, the Spirit of God in us is love, and if the situation requires wisdom or counsel, it is all readily available in us by His Spirit and His Word. We are expected to use what we have got in us to change the situation and not to act helplessly in fear and worry.

When the disciples were threatened not to preach again in the name of Jesus, they didn't go back to their houses to hide and stay quiet until the authorities permitted them to speak again in the name of Jesus. Not at all! The Bible says, *"They went to their own company and reported all that the chief priest* *and elders had said unto them. And when they heard that, they lifted up their voices to God with one accord and said...And now, Lord behold their threatening and grant unto thy servants, that with all <u>boldness</u> they may speak thy word. By stretching forth thine hand to heal and that signs and wonders may be done by the name of thy holy child Jesus. And when they had prayed, the place was shaken where they were assembled together and they were all filled with the Holy Ghost and they spake the word of God with <u>boldness</u>.*" (Acts 4:23-31).

Very remarkable indeed! The disciples, after hearing the threats from the authorities, lifted their hands to pray to the God of all power and authority, asking Him to grant them boldness to speak more in the name of Jesus and perform more miracles for which they had been arrested. Little wonder that the place where they gathered was shaken once more like the day of Pentecost, and they were filled with the Holy Ghost, who is the Spirit of power, love, and of a sound mind. They prayed for boldness because no matter the amount of threats they received, they were determined to take the gospel forward.

If you know the Holy Ghost, you know he is the master of boldness. No one ever got filled with the Holy Ghost and remained timid. It is impossible to have him and be fearful. The Holy Spirit is the ultimate answer to all man's problems. With the Holy Spirit, we are heavily empowered. He is all that we ever needed to rule over situations. Therefore, Paul says, *"Don't be drunk with wine because that will ruin your life. Instead let the Holy Spirit fill and control you."* (Ephesians 5:18-21 NLT).

Our life of faith

Christianity is a life of faith; it has nothing to do with our feelings. Faith is not something we pick up to use whenever we want to get something from the Lord. Faith is yielding our entire self completely over to Christ; walking with God, seeing beyond the physical world; and living life according to the Word of God without fear, apology, or compromise. The New International Version of the Bible defines faith as, *"being sure of what we hope for and certain of what we do not see."* (Hebrews 11:1).

This is exactly what Abraham, the Father of faith, demonstrated when God told him to leave his father's house and go to the land that He would show him. (Genesis 12:1). Abraham believed in God and left his father's house with his wife Sarah and lost his nephew to the land that God would show him. He didn't know where the land was located, but moved in faith to find the land that God was going to show him. He did find the land, and God gave it to him and his descendants. (Genesis 13:14-15).

Faith is total trust in God, choosing above everything to take him at His Word. Abraham was called a friend of God for this very reason. He believed in God (James 2:23). Faith is being confident in your heart that God's Word is final, and then you take the necessary action according to the Word of God. Faith is first of all heard in your words and then seen in your actions. James says faith without action is dead. (James 2:14-26).

When God promised Abraham a son, the Bible says, *"And being not weak in faith he considered not his own body now dead when he was about a hundred years old neither the deadness of Sarah's womb; He staggered not at the promise of God through unbelief but was strong in faith, giving glory to God. And being fully persuaded that what he had promised he was able also to perform."* (Romans 4:19-21).

The promised child was finally born, but while the boy was still young and tender, the Bible says God told Abraham to offer him as a burnt offering. Because Abraham had trained himself to walk with God, he was not going to turn back at this point. He had faith in God, who raises the dead (Hebrews 11:19). Abraham committedly demonstrated a life of faith in God, proving that we can also choose to live a life of faith and prove our total trust in God regardless of the circumstances.

While commissioning Joshua to lead the children of Israel to the land of their inheritance, God told him to be very courageous saying, *"Be strong and of a good courage ... Only be thou strong and very courageous that thou may observe to do according to all the law which Moses my servant commanded thee..."* (Joshua 1:6-7). We must be very strong and very courageous to choose God's Word above everything else, especially in this day. Amid so many voices, we must deliberately choose to trust God and take Him at His Word.

Always remember we are not of this world. We live by a different set of rules. We hear a different sound from our heavenly kingdom, and we match according to that sound. Just like Shadrach, Meshach, and Abednego, we refuse to give in even when the fire is made seven times hotter. (Daniel 3:8-30).

* * *

CHAPTER SIX

Watch and pray

"The end of all things is at hand; therefore be serious and watchful in your prayers." (1 Peter 4:7).

To be serious and watchful in prayer is to pray with knowledge and understanding of the times and what needs to be done. For example, how should we pray at this particular point in time when Bible prophecy is being fulfilled before our own eyes? Apart from praying for ourselves to be found ready, what else should we pray for?

Apostle Paul instructed us by the Spirit saying, *"I exhort therefore, that first of all, supplications, prayers, intercessions, and giving of thanks be made for all men; For kings, and for all that are in authority; <u>that we may lead a quiet and peaceable life in all godliness and honesty</u>. For this is good and acceptable in the sight of God our Savior; Who will have all men to be saved and to come unto the knowledge of the truth; For there is one God and one mediator between God and men the man Christ Jesus. Who gave himself a ransom for all, to be testified in due time."* (1 Tim 2:1-6).

This lets us know how important it is for us to pray for those in leadership first, so we can live a peaceable life and be able to do those things that the master wants us to do before we check out of here. Leaders of nations and geographical territories have a big part to play, given the authority they carry. But we have been empowered to control events from the realm of the spirit. That is why we don't have to simply sit back and wait for our governments to do something; we have to pray for our governments and all our leaders to act wisely.

The times have changed. The forces of evil are more forceful than ever, just to cause destruction to humanity, and their channel is first through the leaders of the people. Therefore, pray for your leaders, that wicked and unreasonable men, men without faith, will be far from them. Pray for God's covering over your land, dispatch the holy angels of God all over your territory and beyond, and paralyze all the activities of the wicked one. We need to do this for the gospel to move forward and be able to rescue many before the time is up.

Secondly, it is good and acceptable before God, who wants all men to be saved. If you have read your Bible well and know what will soon happen to this world, you will want everybody to escape. But they will not escape just because we want them to. God wants everybody to escape more than we do. He didn't plan the coming destruction for man but for the devil and his demons. God has done His part through His son Jesus Christ; He is now counting on all of us, His children, to ensure everyone hears about the way of escape.

Therefore, we must pray for all men around the world whose minds are blinded by the god of this evil world system, who doesn't want them to see the light of this glorious gospel that is shining upon them from everywhere.

Pray that the power of the Holy Spirit will prevail upon their hearts to see and receive the gospel of Christ, which is God's only way of escape. For the Scripture has said, *"How shall we escape if we neglect so great salvation which at the first begun to be spoken by the Lord and was confirmed unto us by them that heard him."* (Hebrews 2:3).

Finally, brothers and sisters, let us watch and pray as the master cautioned us before He left saying, *"Heaven and earth will pass away, but my words will by no means pass away. But take heed to yourselves lest your hearts be weighed down with carousing, drunkenness, and cares of this life; and that day comes on you unexpectedly. For it will come as a snare on all those who dwell on the face of the whole earth. Watch therefore and pray always that you may be counted worthy to escape all these things that will come to pass and stand before the son of man."* (Luke 21:33-36).

* * *

CHAPTER SEVEN Prayer of Salvation

In case you have been reading this book and you are not yet born again, or you have walked away from the faith, now is the time to put things right with God. We believe this is your appointed time to receive this precious gift of eternal life and start a personal relationship with God Almighty by wholeheartedly repeating the confession below:

Dear Father, thank you for loving me so much that you sent your only begotten son; that if I believe in him, I should never perish but have everlasting life.

Father as Your Word says that if we shall confess with our mouth the Lord Jesus and shall believe in our hearts that You have raised him from the dead, we shall be saved According to Romans 10:9; I right now confess with my mouth that Jesus is my lord and savior because I believe in my heart that he died for me and You raised him from the dead for my salvation.

Thank You, dear father, for saving my life and for the precious gift of eternal life I have received now through Jesus Christ. Declare that I am born again. I am Your child with Your nature and life in me.

I belong to Your kingdom now. I am a new creature, the old is gone, the new has come, and all the new in me now is from You, my God, in Jesus' mighty name. Amen.

Congratulations! You are now a child of God. You can reach us for more information through the contact address in this book. God richly bless you!

* * *